DEEP IN IT
PREQUEL: GROWN WOMAN CHRONICLES

MICHELLE DAVIS

CONTENTS

Nobody	1
Offer	2
Fight	4
I Deserve	6
I Should Have Listened	7
Life Keeps Moving	10
Encompassing	12
Never Enough	13
Untitled	16
Staged Panties	18
She is Not Me, I am Not Her	20
Situationship	21
Rebound	22
Who Beholds Me?	25
He said, I said	27
Where has Black Love Gone?	29
Best of Me	31
My Offer Still Stands	33
Someone New	35
Side Chick with a Side Eye	37
It's Me Not You	40
I'm Sorry	42

Independently Published

Copyright © 2020 MICHELLE **DAVIS**

All rights reserved. No part of this publication may be reproduced, stored in or introduced into a retrieval system, or transmitted, in any form or by any means, electronic, mechanical, photocopying, recording or otherwise without the prior written consent of the copyright owner.

ISBN: 978-1-954613-06-5

Cover Art: selfpubbookcovers.com/BeeJavier

"When love knocks you down, get back up. Take time to heal, reflect, but never give up. Keep loving and know you are better, stronger, and wiser because of your experiences." -Michelle Davis

NOBODY

Nobody loves me
Nobody cares for me
Who are you to love me now?

Nobody listens
I am only a voice in the wind
Flowing, rolling over heads, and over skin

My heart whimpers
Swelling with love, wanting to give, but receiving none

Lost in a crowd, feet planted on the ground, but I am not grounded

OFFER

You offered me the best of you

I told you about everything I had been through

You said you wanted me to see, how happy and in love we could be

I told you I was not ready to be a girlfriend, lover, or companion

You heard my voice but not my words

Took it upon yourself to make me yours

You grabbed my hand and said follow your lead

I held on tight, took caution, and heed

I opened my heart because you said trust

I opened my mind because you said I must

In order to come on this journey with you I had to give my all

You explained to me the importance of being open to love

You explained to me the importance of understanding the desires of my heart

I heard you, understood you, and allowed you to be a part

I hope you understand I am trying to believe

You took my hand and said you would navigate until I can see

Through the haze, confusion, and misery

To a place of love and security

Exploring all our possibilities

I am open to love

FIGHT

I can't be the only one
I can't do this alone

If this relationship is going to work, we need to unite, we need to fight

Not about the issues, not about each other, but for each other

We need to think about life
Think about love

Think about the words we shared when we made the commitment in front of family, friends, and our Lord above

We committed to love, honor, and respect each other

Be there through sickness and health

We dated, broke up, and made up

Cried, healed and made the decision to seal the deal

This relationship is not just about love, it is about the journey
A work in progress, a story to unfold

Each time we begin to lose sight we need to remember that in life there are times we need to fight

No fist
No guns
No words of abuse

Remembering what is at stake
Getting the courage to admit our mistakes

Realizing we are stronger and happier together
There isn't any storm we can't weather, if we remember to fight

I DESERVE

Words mean nothing to me when your actions are meant to destroy me

My demeanor reflects your behavior inflicted upon me

Why are you hurting? Why are you hurting me?

Your perception of your circumstance, and your lack of confidence is revealed in how you treat me

As your better half, as the best part of you, I deserve better than what I am getting

I SHOULD HAVE LISTENED

A little birdie
A friend of a friend
The grapevine

I should have listened when the world was trying to tell me about you

The other women
Your "boys"
Strangers in the street

Wanted me to know you were behaving and conducting yourself in whorish ways

Never one to partake in gossip

Never wanting to take someone else's word

I hid, avoiding anyone or anywhere the rumors could penetrate me

When the accusations became too visible, I put on the protective shades you had given me

Rose colored, gold encrusted, only allowing me to view the situation from your perspective

As my telephone rang, the sirens sang about your newest acquisition

Awareness of your transgressions made my stomach churn

In an overload of my senses, my head began to hurt, and my eyes began to burn

The shades could not protect me
Your infidelity was all around me

Blinders off, armed with information, I now had to face reality

My intuition kicked in, and I caught you red handed

She was in your bed, like everyone said

Yelling at me, cursing me out like I was the other woman and you were her man

I will remember this day all my life

No explanation required; no excuses needed

I put my big girl panties on; my fault, I should have listened

LIFE KEEPS MOVING

You are talking to me like you know me
I keep telling you I have changed

I am not the same chick you once knew
Fall back, stay in your lane

Stop trying to pick up where we left off

I keep telling you too much has happened

You left me, and expect me to come back to you like no time was ever lost

Life keeps moving

Time doesn't stop

I think in your head time stood still
In your mind, I am still yours

I keep telling you I am not the same girl you knew
I grew up and got over you

ENCOMPASSING

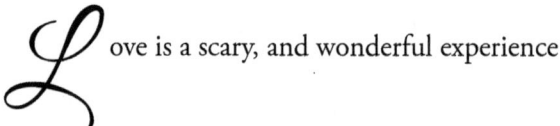ove is a scary, and wonderful experience

To be in love, to give love, to acknowledge, and receive love

To be open to rejection, acceptance, and redemption

Uncertain of the outcome, continue to endure

NEVER ENOUGH

Neck on a swivel
    Checking out everything that walks by
I never thought you would have a wandering eye

Disappointed
I can't believe what I just saw

Watching you look at her specifically, open mouth, eyes in awe

Mouth open, eyes glazed over
Like an animal ready to pounce
I caught you in full on lust

. . .

What were you thinking about her?

Do you think she is going to put up with you?

Your stank attitude

Your bad mood

Your stubbornness

Frequent moments of being rude

What caught your attention?

Was it her fresh face and ivory skin?

Was it her brown razor cut hair, and that her body was stick thin?

Help me, please elaborate, I just don't understand

She looks nothing like me, but you are drooling

Don't toss me a line that you are 'just being a man'

You should have more respect for your lady, and best friend

Let me share with you a little secret, just in case you didn't know

If you can't control your eyes you will leave your key, and be walked out the door

. . .

A real man controls his impulses, has respect, and isn't easily influenced

I must ask myself; whose boy am I nursing?

UNTITLED

I hate the way I feel whenever you are around

You make me sad, you bring me down

Often, I can't catch my breath; I feel like I am going to drown

No peace of mind, I need some time

To think
Love myself
Dream

Smothered, I feel like running away

. . .

To a place where I can enact fantasies and be my true self

Roll around in grass, meditate, and pray

I want to stare into space for long periods of time

Contemplating existence and who I will be in the next lifetime

I am energy

I am love

I am positivity

You keep me tame with your negativity

Erupting with anger, I am breaking free

Come with me, join my way of living or lose me to my ingenuity

STAGED PANTIES

Yes, I know about you, I see you all the time
When I am with him, I can always tell when you are on his mind

I see it in his eyes when he looks at me, he sees me, but remembering you

When he reaches out to kiss me, his lips feel depleted, dry, and exhausted from your visit last night

By the way, I got the message you left in the bathroom

I saw your makeup on his towel, and caught the smell of your perfume

You want me to solve the puzzle, you want me to acknowledge you

You see me with him, you know about me, but you wonder if I know about you

I found your hair in his sheets, hard to dismiss

You must be tired of being ignored, I found your bombshell hint

As I was gathering my belongings walking out the door

He stopped me and said I forgot something in his dresser drawer

He handed me a pair of size 8 panties

Too bad I wear a size 4

SHE IS NOT ME, I AM NOT HER

Why does it bother me to see her with you?

You and I were not compatible

We tried to make it work

I just don't understand why I get upset when I see her with you

Is it because she is everything you always tried to tell me I should be?

Is it because in her I see everything you complained about in me?

Is she like the bride of Frankenstein, I must see the monster?

Is she your creation from your dreams, and fantasies?

I know for sure it is not you I want nor her I desire to be

I guess for now I must contend with letting curiosity get the best of me

SITUATIONSHIP

We were never meant to be
We were just fulfilling each other's needs
No compatibility, love, or connection
A relationship ensued based on adoration and affection
Loneliness, confusion, just wanting someone to hold
It started off innocent, and became co-dependent
One day reality set in
We realized there was no commitment
Grabbing our belongings and going our separate ways
We knew this had to end someday

REBOUND

The definition of insanity is doing the same thing over and over, expecting different results

Are we insane?

Based on what we have been doing I think we are beyond insanity, heading towards bat shit crazy

Why do I think I can change you?
And you think you can change me?

Why are we still in this relationship when we both know this is not where we want to be?

Why can't we let go?

Why can't we say no, and walk away?

Are we waiting for the right one to come, take our hearts, and whisk us away?

Why do we continue to stay?

Together
Broken
Mentally wrecked in this bad situation

Why are we so afraid of being alone?

Why are we willing to be miserable, unloved, and unsatisfied?
Just to be able to say we are in a relationship?

Pressured by restaurant seating charts
Reservations for two
Couple trips
Holidays
Double dates and social events

I would rather be by myself, wait, and meet someone great

I pride myself on my sensibility

I want to keep my sanity

This relationship with you is not the best for me

What we are doing is not healthy

Let's make a commitment today to be single and free
Living life and allowing space for our destiny

WHO BEHOLDS ME?

Beauty is in the eye of the beholder
    Who beholds me?

My beauty is unique shown in my mystique

Mahogany brown skin

Youthful glow

Seductive walk

Tantalizing talk

Insatiable appetite for love

Quaint idea of life

Unbridled enthusiasm

Cultivated mind

I am not the average woman, I am a lady

        . . .

A true gem

Natural not manufactured

Dressed up to play the part

Get to know me

My likes, dislikes

My desires, passions

My sensuality, not my sexuality

My beauty, not my appearance

In these times of materialism, and image consciousness

Who beholds me?

HE SAID, I SAID

He *said*

I was a plain Jane

Too smart

A know it all

Thought too highly of myself

Wasn't feminine enough

I *said*

I am naturally beautiful

Knowledgeable from experience

Secure in myself, and my identity

Strong from my ancestral mothers

He *said*

I was distant

Untrusting

Uncompromising

Judgmental

I *said*

I am protective of myself, and my heart

Trust should be earned, and reciprocated in return

I want the best for myself, and my mate, and will not settle for less

Through his actions he showed me my strength, and displayed his weaknesses, he cheated, and it was my fault

Always pushing him to be his best, never settling for less

Giving him love, not just sex

Being a friend by telling him the truth about himself; the good and the bad

I took a deep breath, and collected my thoughts and this is what **I *said***

Celebrate my beauty, admire my strength,

I am not the cause of your flaws

You will not blame me for your poor decisions

Take ownership of your indiscretions

You made a mistake, one that has repercussions

As I turned and walked out the door on his face, I saw strife

I *said*, the relationship is over, have a happy life

WHERE HAS BLACK LOVE GONE?

Where has black love gone

    Sown in the depths of a midnight song

Painfully lost in societies exploitation

We have forgotten the pledge of love, and dedication

The hurt, the search, the insecurity of love

The hunger for affection leads us to degradation

Forget the man in the mirror— it's the girl in the video

Who does not mind being called…eye candy, yeah that's what she's called

With the brother on the corner playing undercover

Down low, yeah that's what he's called

Love is love, and lust is lust

Recognizing what you have is a must

Be true to yourself, and the desires of your heart

Respect one another, don't tear each other apart

BEST OF ME

I can't be a piece of ass

Breast of pillows

Bottle of nipples to pacify you

I won't be fingers to soothe you

Rub you

Massage your pain away

I will not be an erotic toy

A hit without a kiss

An oven to keep your manhood warm

No passion

No depth

Just moans of lust and physical arabesque

There is more to me if you take the time to see; I am offering you the best of me

I can be your homegirl, friend to the end

I can be a good listener, someone to confide in

I could be a guide into a world where anything is possible

Feel honored and blessed that I have decided to give you my best

I can't be, won't be just some chick

You could be but I won't allow you to be just some dick

What you and I could be are friends

A friend is what I can be if you would take the time to see

I am offering you the best of me

MY OFFER STILL STANDS

I offered you the best of me

You asked me what I thought we could be

You were the one who wanted to see where things could go and if this thing, we had could grow

I opened my heart because you said trust

I opened my mind because you said I must

In order to come on this journey with you I had to give my all

You've been hurt and I am sorry for that but hurting me won't

Bring her back

Soothe your pain

Make you a better man

Again, my offer still stands

You are chasing me, I am not chasing you

This is all because you saw something you wanted to pursue

Understand, this is not about catching a feeling

It's about the fact that I came into this situation willing to explore the possibilities of you, and I

The possibility to be in love, and to give love

Embrace the cries of your heart yearning for my love

Take my hand, my offer still stands

Follow my lead until you are able to see

Through the haze, confusion, and misery

To a place of love, and possibility

My offer still stands

SOMEONE NEW

I am okay, Boo, that you found someone new

Your decision tells me your leg on my journey is done, and through

Please understand and let me make it clear that my feelings toward you, and your someone new are true, and sincere

Everything happens for a reason though we may not understand

No need to look up me up or ring my phone when you realize I made you a better man

Just respect my space, and remember I had grace when I let you go, without spectacle

No need to exchange rings or separate things

What's yours is yours, what's mine is mine

Gifts are gifts so don't even trip

Amicably, and peacefully we ended our relationship

No fussin' or cussin'

I pulled out all the class I could muster

Bye Bye

See you later

Catch you on the flip

I sincerely hope you will take time to heal, and are not riding on the rebound bus with your new chick

I will never be her, and she will never be me

I am happy to no longer be swinging from the silly tree

What our future holds, I guess we will have to wait, and see

My hope is blessings for you, and of course blessings for me

Because as I stated I am okay, boo, because in the end it was your choice to find someone new

SIDE CHICK WITH A SIDE EYE

I see you looking
    Over there cutting me with your eyes

I see you watching

Trying to figure out how you can claim the prize

I see you stalking

Trying to be everywhere he's going to be

Don't try to befriend me

Trying to get information from the inside

I'm on to your game

You're a hood rat groupie lacking class

I think you're lame

You better not even think about saying his name

I called your bluff

All of a sudden you acting tough

You're a disgrace

Telling him don't worry he can meet you at your place

The jokes on you

I don't know why you're so surprised

I thought you knew

You're nothing but the side chick with a side eye

Snitch

Dude in the shadows

Wing man on the side

You are always with him

Always along for the ride

Telling me his secrets

Adding your words on the sly

Telling me he is not your friend just an acquaintance

You are coming to me, and going back to him

I don't trust you

Don't know you

Be real

I am not your girl

Go get a life

I don't have any respect for you or your crew

Trying to get with me but I don't want you

Stop snitching and creeping

Dude go get a life

I don't trust you

Don't respect you

You are a snitch, you and your crew

IT'S ME NOT YOU

The problem is me not you
Such a cliché but true
I'm not feeling the way you do
It's not right for me to put you through
My confusion
Indecision
Nonchalance
It's just not fair
You are always calling me
Wanting to see me
I can't breathe, I need some air
Most women would love a man like you
I just want this to be done, and through

Don't change who you are for me

I am just not the right woman for you, and you and I are not meant to be

I'M SORRY

There is no making up for what you did

Saying you're sorry can't repair the damage

I can't believe you think that's all it takes to put the pieces of my heart back together

The heart you love to break

It's a constant theme in this relationship

I'm sorry, please forgive me

I take you back each and every time

Until the next time

When I catch you messing with some whore

You then spend the night outside knocking, and apologizing at my door

'I'm sorry' doesn't cut it

I just can't take anymore

I am tired, embarrassed, and believe I am worth so much more

I am not what you want, you are not what I need

Go take your apologizes to the next chick

I am sorry but I am moving on

www.ingramcontent.com/pod-product-compliance
Lightning Source LLC
Chambersburg PA
CBHW061302040426
42444CB00010B/2486